Statements

Occasional Papers of the Phelps-Stokes Fund

This Past Must Address Its Present
The 1986 Nobel Lecture

Wole Soyinka

D1264014

Number 3   **March 1988**

Wole Soyinka

Wole Soyinka received the Nobel Prize for Literature in 1986. In its announcement, the Swedish Academy cited the work of the Nigerian playwright and poet "who in a wide cultural perspective and with poetic overtones fashions the drama of existence."

Wole Soyinka was born at Abeokuta, in western Nigeria, on July 13, 1934. He was educated at University College, Ibadan, Nigeria, and the University of Leeds, England, where (in 1973) he received his doctorate. From 1958 to 1959 Soyinka worked as a dramaturgist at the Royal Court Theatre in London. As a result of an article appealing for a cease-fire in Nigeria's civil war, Soyinka was accused of conspiring with the Biafra rebels, arrested, and held as a political prisoner from 1967 to 1969. He has taught drama and literature at the universities of Ibadan, Lagos, and Ife, where he is currently professor of comparative literature, and as a visiting professor at Cambridge, Sheffield, and Yale.

Soyinka's published works, written in English, include plays, poetry, novels, and essays. Among his plays are *The Swamp Dwellers* (1958); *The Lion and the Jewel* (1959); *The Trials of Brother Jero* (1960) and *Jero's Metamorphosis* (1973); *A Dance of the Forests* (1960); *The Strong Breed* (1963); *Kongi's Harvest* (1965); *The Road* (1965); *Madmen and Specialists* (1970); *The Bacchae of Euripides* (1973); *Death and the King's Horseman* (1975); *Opera Wonyosi* (1977); *A Play of Giants* (1984); and *Requiem for a Futurologist* (1985). Volumes of poetry are *Idanre, and Other Poems* (1967); *Poems from Prison* (1969); *A Shuttle in the Crypt* (1972); and *Ogun Abibman* (1976). His prose works include the novels *The Interpreters* (1965) and *Season of Anomy* (1973); the autobiographical *The Man Died: Prison Notes* (1972) and *Aké: The Years of Childhood* (1981); and essays collected under the title *Myth, Literature, and the African World*.

—Ronald Austin Wells

I will stand here for humanity. . . .
–Ralph Waldo Emerson

This Past Must Address Its Present

Dedicated to Nelson Mandela

A RATHER CURIOUS scene, unscripted, once took place in the wings of a London theater at the same time as the scheduled performance was being presented on the actual stage, before an audience. What happened was this: an actor refused to come on stage for his allocated role. Action was suspended. A fellow actor tried to persuade him to emerge, but he stubbornly shook his head. Then a struggle ensued. The second actor had hoped that, suddenly exposed to the audience in full glare of the spotlight, the reluctant actor would have no choice but to rejoin the cast. And so he tried to take the delinquent actor by surprise, pulling him suddenly toward the stage. He did not fully succeed, so a brief but untidy struggle began. The unwilling actor was completely taken aback and deeply embarrassed—some of that tussle was quite visible to a part of the audience.

The performance itself, it should be explained, was an improvisation around an incident. This meant that the actors were free—within the convention of the performance—to stop, rework any part they wished, invite members of the audience on stage, assign roles, and change costumes in full view of the audience. They therefore could also dramatize their wish to have that uncooperative actor join them—which they did with gusto. That actor had indeed left the stage before the contentious scene began. He had served notice during rehearsals that he would not participate in it. In the end, he had his way, but the incident proved very troubling to him for weeks afterward. He found himself compelled to puzzle out this clash in attitudes between himself and his fellow writers and performers. He experienced, on the one hand, an intense rage that he had been made to appear incapable of confronting a stark reality, made to appear to suffer from interpretative coyness, to seem inhibited by a cruel reality or perhaps to carry his emotional involvement with an

1

event so far as to interfere with his professional will. Of course, he knew that it was none of these things. The truth was far simpler. Unlike his colleagues, together with whom he shared, unquestionably, the same political attitude toward the event that was being represented, he found the mode of presentation at war with the ugliness it tried to convey, creating an intense disquiet about his very presence on that stage, in that place, before an audience whom he considered collectively responsible for that dehumanizing actuality.

And now let us remove some of the mystery and make that incident a little more concrete. The scene was the Royal Court Theatre, London, 1958. It was one of those Sunday nights that were given to experimentation, an innovation of that remarkable theater manager-director George Devine, whose creative nurturing radicalized British theater of that period and produced later icons like John Osborne, N.F. Simpson, Edward Bond, Arnold Wesker, Harold Pinter, and John Arden and even forced the then conservative British palate to sample stylistic and ideological pariahs like Samuel Beckett and Bertolt Brecht. On this particular occasion, the evening was devoted to a form of "living" theater, and the main fare was titled *Eleven Men Dead at Hola*. The actors were not all professional actors; indeed they were mostly writers who jointly created and performed these dramatic pieces. Those with a long political memory may recall what took place at Hola Camp, Kenya, during the Mau-Mau liberation struggle. The British colonial power believed that the Mau-Mau could be smashed by herding Kenyans into special camps, trying to separate the hard cases, the mere suspects, and the potential recruits—oh, they had it all neatly worked out. One such camp was Hola Camp—and the incident involved the death of eleven of the detainees, who were simply beaten to death by camp officers and warders. The usual inquiry set up, and it was indeed the report that provided the main text on which the performance was based.

We need now only identify the reluctant actor and, if you have not guessed by now, he was none other than this speaker. I recall the occasion as vividly as actors are wont to recollect forever and ever the frightening moment of a blackout, when not only the lines are forgotten but even the moment in the play. The role that I had been assigned was that of a camp guard, one of the killers. We were equipped with huge nightsticks and, while a narrator read the testimony of one of the guards, our task was to raise the cudgels slowly and, almost ritualistically, bring them down on the necks and shoulders of the prisoners, under the orders of the white camp officers. A surreal scene. Even in rehearsals, it was clear that the end product would be a surrealist tableau. The narrator at a lectern under a spot; a dispassionate reading, deliberately clinical, letting the stark facts reveal the states of mind of torturers and victims. A small ring of white officers, armed. One seizes a cudgel from one of the warders to demonstrate how to beat a human being without leaving visible marks. Then the innermost clump of detainees, their only weapon nonviolence. They had taken their decision to go on strike, refused to go to work unless they obtained better camp conditions. So they squatted on the ground and refused to move, locked their hands behind their knees in silent defiance. Orders were given. The inner ring of guards, the blacks, moved in, lifted their bodies by hooking hands underneath the armpits of the detainees, carried them like toads in a state of petrification to one side, divided them in groups.

The faces of the victims are impassive; they are resolved to offer no resistance. The beatings begin: one to the left side, then the back, the arms—right, left, front, back. Rhythmically. The cudgels swing in unison. The faces of the white guards glow with professional satisfaction, their arms gesture languidly from time to time, suggesting it is time to shift to the next batch or beat a little more severely on the neglected side. In terms of images, a fluid, near balletic scene.

Then the contrast, the earlier official version, enacting how the prisoners were supposed to have died. This claimed that the prisoners had collapsed, that they died after drinking from a poisoned water supply. So we staged that also. The prisoners filed to the water wagon, gasping with thirst. After the first two or three had drunk and commenced writhing with pain, these humane guards rushed to stop the others, but no, they were already wild with thirst, fought their way past salvation, and drank greedily from the same source. The groans spread from one to the other, the writhing, the collapse—the agonized deaths. That was the version of the camp governors.

The motif was simple enough, the theatrical format a tried and tested one, faithful to a particular convention. What then was the problem? It was one, I believe, that affects most writers. When is playacting rebuked by reality? When is fictionalizing presumptuous? What happens

3

after playacting? One of the remarkable properties of the particular theatrical convention I have just described is that it gives off a strong odor of perenniality, that feeling of "I have been here before," "I have been witness to this," "The past enacts its presence." In such an instance, that sense of perenniality can serve both as exorcism, a certificate of release, and indeed—especially for the audience—a soporific. We must bear in mind that at the time of presentation, and to the major part of that audience, every death of a freedom fighter was a notch on a gun, the death of a fiend, an animal, a bestial mutant, not the martyrdom of a patriot.

We know also, however, that such efforts can provoke changes, that an actualization of the statistical, journalistic footnote can arouse revulsion in the complacent mind, leading to the beginning of a commitment to change, redress. And on this occasion, angry questions had been raised in the houses of Parliament. Liberals, humanitarians, and reformists had taken up the cause of justice for the victims. Some had even traveled to Kenya to obtain details that exposed the official lie. This profound unease, which paralyzed my creative will, therefore reached beyond the audience, and, finally, I traced its roots to my own feelings of assaulted humanity, which clamored for a different form of response. It provoked a feeling of indecency about that presentation, rather like the deformed arm of a leper that is thrust at the healthy to provoke a charitable sentiment. This, I believe, was the cause of that intangible but totally visceral rejection which thwarted the demands of my calling, rendered it inadequate, and mocked the empathy of my colleagues. It was as if the inhuman totality, of which that scene was a mere fragment, was saying to us: Kindly keep your comfortable sentiment to yourselves.

Of course, I utilize that episode only as illustration of the far deeper internalized processes of the creative mind, a process that endangers the writer in two ways: he either freezes up completely or abandons the pen for far more direct means of contesting unacceptable reality. And again, Hola Camp provides a convenient means of approaching that aspect of my continent's reality which, for us whom it directly affronts, constitutes the greatest threat to global peace in our actual existence. For there is a gruesome appropriateness in the fact that an African, a black man, should stand here today, in the same year that the progressive prime minister of this host country was murdered, in the same year as Samora Machel was brought down on the territory of the desperate last-ditch

4

guardians of the theory of racial superiority, which has brought so much misery to our common humanity. Whatever the facts are about Olof Palme's death, there can be no question about his life. To the racial oppression of a larger sector of humanity, Olof Palme pronounced, and acted, a decisive No! Perhaps it was those who were outraged by this act of racial "treachery" who were myopic enough to imagine that the death of an individual would arrest the march of his convictions; perhaps his murder was simply yet another instance of the terror epidemic that feeds today on shock, not reason. It does not matter; an authentic conscience of the white tribe has been stilled, and the loss is both yours and mine. Samora Machel, the leader who once placed his country on a war footing against South Africa, went down in as yet mysterious circumstances. True, we are all still haunted by the Nkomati Accord, which negated that earlier triumphant moment of the African collective will; nevertheless, his foes across the border have good reason to rejoice over his demise, and, in that sense, his death is, ironically, a form of triumph for the black race.

Is that perhaps too stark a paradox? Then let me take you back to Hola Camp. It is cattle that are objects of the stick, or whip. So are horses, goats, donkeys, and so on. Their definition therefore involves occasionally being beaten to death. If, thirty years after Hola Camp, it is at all thinkable that it takes the ingenuity of the most sophisticated electronic interference to kill an African resistance fighter, the champions of racism are already admitting to themselves what they continue to deny to the world: that they, white supremacist breed, have indeed come a long way in their definition of their chosen enemy since Hola Camp. They have come an incredibly long way since Sharpeville, when they shot unarmed, fleeing Africans in the back. They have come very far since 1930, when in the first such organized incident, the South African blacks decided to turn Dingaan's Day, named for the defeat of the Zulu leader Dingaan, into a symbol of affirmative resistance by publicly destroying their obnoxious passes. In response to those thousands of passes burned on Cartright Flats, the Durban police descended on the unarmed protesters, killing some half dozen and wounding hundreds. They backed their action up with a scorched-earth campaign that dispersed thousands of Africans from their normal environment, victims of imprisonment and deportation. And even that 1930 repression was a

5

quantum leap from that earlier, spontaneous protest against the native-pass law in 1919 when the police merely rode down the protesters on horseback, whipped and sjamboked them, chased and harried them likè stray goats and wayward cattle, from street corner to shanty lodge. Every act of racial terror, with its vastly increasing sophistication of style and escalation in human loss, is itself an acknowledgment of improved knowledge of, and respect for, the potential of what is feared, an acknowledgement of the sharpening tempo of triumph by the victimized.

For there was this aspect that struck me most forcibly in that attempt to re-create the crime at Hola Camp; in the various testimonies of the white officers, it stuck out, whether stated overtly or simply through their efficient detachment from the ongoing massacre. It was this: at no time did these white overseers actually experience the human "otherness" of their victims. They clearly did not experience the reality of the victims as human beings. Animals perhaps, a noxious form of vegetable life maybe, but certainly not human. I do not speak here of their colonial overlords, the ones who formulated and sustained the policy of settler colonialism, the ones who dispatched the Maxim guns and tuned the imperial bugle. They knew very well that empires existed that had to be broken, that centuries-old civilizations endured that had to be destroyed. The "subhuman" denigration for which their "civilizing mission" became the altruistic remedy was the mere rationalizing icing on the cake of imperial greed. But yes indeed, there were the agents, those who carried out orders (like Eichmann, to draw parallels from the white continent); they—whether as bureaucrats, technicians, or camp governors—had no conceptual space in their heads that could be filled, except very rarely and exceptionally, by "the black as *also* human." It would be correct to say that this has remained the pathology of the average South African white since the turn of the last century to this moment. Here, for example, is one frank admission by an enlightened, even radical mind of that country:

> *It was not until my last year in school that it had occurred to me that these black people, these voteless masses, were in any way concerned with the socialism which I professed or that they had any role to play in the great social revolution which in these days seemed to be*

imminent. The "workers" who were destined to inherit the new world were naturally the white carpenters and bricklayers, the tramworkers and miners who were organized in their trade unions and who voted for the Labour Party. I would no more have thought of discussing politics with a native youth than of inviting him home to play with me or to a meal or asking him to join the Carnarvon Football Club. The African was on a different plane, hardly human, part of the scene as were dogs and trees and, more remotely, cows. I had no special feelings about him, not interest nor hate nor love. He just did not come into my social picture. So completely had I accepted the traditional attitudes of the time.

Yes, I believe that this self-analysis by Eddie Roux, the Afrikaaner political rebel and scientist, remains today the flat, unvarnished truth for the majority of Afrikaaners. "No special feelings, . . . not interest nor hate nor love," the result of a complete acceptance of "traditional attitudes." That passage captures a mind's racial *tabula rasa*, if you like, in the first decade of this century, about the time, in short, when the Nobel series of prizes was inaugurated. But a slate, no matter how clean, cannot avoid receiving impressions once it is exposed to air—fresh or polluted. And we are now in the year 1986, that is, after an entire century of direct, intimate exposure since that confrontation, that first rejection of the dehumanizing label implicit in the native-pass laws.

Eddie Roux, like hundreds, even thousands of his countrymen, soon made rapid strides. His race has produced its list of martyrs in the cause of non-racialism—one remembers, still with a tinge of pain, Ruth First, destroyed by a letter bomb delivered by the long arm of apartheid. There are others—Andre Brink, Abram Fischer, Helen Suzman, Breyten Breytenbach—with the scars of martyrdom still seared into their souls. Intellectuals, writers, scientists, plain workingmen, politicians— they come to that point where a social reality can no longer be observed as a culture on a slide beneath the microscope or turned into aesthetic variations on pages, canvas, or the stage. The blacks, of course, are locked into an unambiguous condition: on this occasion I do not need to address *us*. We know, and we embrace our mission. It is the *other* that this precedent seizes the opportunity to address, and not merely those who are trapped within the confines of that doomed camp but those who

7

live outside, on the fringes of conscience. Those specifically who, with shameless smugness, invent arcane moral propositions that enable them to plead inaction in a language of unparalleled political flatulence: "Personally, I find sanctions morally repugnant." Or what shall we say of another leader for whom economic sanctions that work against an Eastern European country will not work in the apartheid enclave of South Africa, that master of histrionics who takes to the world's airwaves to sing, "Let Poland be," but turns off his hearing aid when the world shouts, "Let Nicaragua be." But enough of these world leaders of double-talk and multiple moralities.

It is baffling to any mind that pretends to the slightest claim to rationality, it is truly and formidably baffling. Can the same terrain of phenomenal assimilation—that is, one that produced evidence of a capacity to translate empirical observations into implications of rational human conduct—can this same terrain that, over half a century ago, fifty entire years, two, three generations ago, produced the Buntings, the Roux, the Douglas Woltons, Solly Sachs, the Gideon Bothas, can that same terrain, fifty, sixty, even seventy years later, be peopled by a species of humanity so ahistorical that the declaration, so clearly spelled out in 1919 at the burning of the passes, remains only a troublesome event of no enduring significance?

Some atavistic bug is at work here that defies all scientific explanation, an arrest in time within the evolutionary mandate of nature that puts all human experience of learning to serious question! We have to ask ourselves, then, what event can speak to such a breed of people? How do we reactivate that petrified cell which houses historic apprehension and development? Is it possible perhaps that events, gatherings such as this, might help? Dare we skirt the edge of hubris and say to them: Take a good look. Provide your response. In your anxiety to prove that this moment is not possible, you have killed, maimed, silenced, tortured, exiled, debased, and dehumanized hundreds of thousands encased in this very skin, crowned with such hair, proudly content with their very being. How many potential partners in the science of heart transplant have you wasted? How do we know how many black South African scientists and writers would have stood here, by now, if you had had the vision to educate the rest of the world in the value of a great multiracial society?

8

Jack Cope surely sums it up in his foreword to *The Adversary Within*, a study of dissidence in Afrikaaner literature, when he states:

> *Looking back from the perspective of the present, I think it can justly be said that, at the core of the matter, the Afrikaaner leaders in 1924 took the wrong turning. Themselves the victims of imperialism in its most evil aspect, all their sufferings and enormous loss of life nevertheless failed to convey to them the obvious historical lesson. They became themselves the new imperialists. They took over from Britain the mantle of empire and colonialism. They could well have set their faces against annexation, aggression, colonial exploitation and oppression, racial arrogance and barefaced hypocrisy, of which they had been themselves the victims. They could have opened the doors to humane ideas and civilizing processes and transformed the great territory with its incalculable resources into another New World. Instead they deliberately set the clock back wherever they could. Taking over ten million indigenous subjects from British colonial rule, they stripped them of what limited rights they had gained over a century and tightened the screws on their subjection.*

Well, perhaps the wars against Chaka and Dingaan and Diginswayo, even the Great Trek, were then too fresh in your *laager* memory. But we are saying that over a century has passed since then, a century in which the world has leapt, in comparative tempo with the past, at least three centuries. And we have seen the potential of man and woman—of all races—contend with the most jealously guarded sovereignty of nature and the cosmos. In every field, both in the humanities and in the sciences, we have seen that human creativity has confronted and tempered the hostility of the environment, adapting, moderating, converting, harmonizing, and even subjugating. Triumphing over errors and resuming the surrendered fields, when man has had time to lick his wounds and listen again to the urgings of his spirit. Distorted, opportunistic renderings of history have been cleansed and restored to truthful reality, because the traducers of the history of others have discovered that the further they advanced, the more their very progress was checked and vitiated by the lacunae they had purposefully inserted in the history of others. Self-interest dictated yet another round of revisionism—slight, niggardly

9

concessions to begin with. But a breach had been made in the dam, and an avalanche has proved the logical progression. From the heart of jungles, even before the aid of high-precision cameras mounted on orbiting satellites, civilizations have resurrected, documenting their own existence with unassailable iconography and art. More amazing still, the records of the ancient voyagers, the merchant adventurers of the age when Europe did not yet require to dominate territories in order to feed its industrial mills—those objective recitals of mariners and adventurers from antiquity confirmed what the archaeological remains affirmed so loudly. They spoke of living communities that regulated their own lives, that had evolved a working relationship with nature, that ministered to their own wants and secured their future with their own genius. These narratives, uncluttered by the impure motives that needed to mystify the plain self-serving rush to dismantle independent societies for easy plundering, pointed accusing fingers unerringly in the direction of European savants, philosophers, scientists, and theorists of human evolution. Gobineau is a notorious name, but how many students of European thought today, even among us Africans, recall that several of the most revered names in European philosophy—Hegel, Locke, Hume, Voltaire—an endless list, were unabashed theorists of racial superiority and denigrators of the African history and being. As for the more prominent names among the theorists of revolution and class struggle—we will draw the curtain of extenuation on their own intellectual aberration, forgiving them a little for their vision of an end to human exploitation.

In any case, the purpose is not really to indict the past but to summon it to the attention of a suicidal, anachronistic present. To say to that mutant present: You are a child of those centuries of lies, distortion, and opportunism in high places, even among the holy of holies of intellectual objectivity. But the world is growing up, while you willfully remain a child, a stubborn, self-destructive child, with certain destructive powers, but a child nevertheless. And to say to the world, to call attention to its own historic passage of lies—as yet unabandoned by some—which sustains the evil precocity of this child. Wherein then lies the surprise that we, the victims of that intellectual dishonesty of others, demand a measure of expiation from that world which is finally coming to itself? Demand that it rescue itself, by concrete acts, from the stigma of being the willful parent of a monstrosity, especially as that monstrous child still draws material nourishment, breath, and human recognition from the strengths and devises of that world, with an umbilical cord that stretches across oceans, even across the cosmos via so-called programs of techno-logical cooperation. We are saying very simply but urgently: Sever that cord. By any name, be it total sanction, boycott, disinvestment, or whatever, sever this umbilical cord and leave this monster of a birth to atrophy and die or to rebuild itself on long-denied humane foundations. Let it collapse, shorn of its external sustenance, let it collapse of its own social disequilibrium, its economic lopsidedness, its war of attrition on its most productive labor. Let it wither like an aborted fetus of the human family if it persists in smothering the minds and sinews that constitute its authentic being.

This pariah society that is apartheid South Africa plays many games on human intelligence. Listen to this, for example. When the whole world escalated its appeal for the release of Nelson Mandela, the South African government blandly declared that it continued to hold Nelson Mandela for the same reasons that the Allied powers continued to hold Rudolf Hess! Now a statement like that is an obvious appeal to the love of the ridiculous in everyone. Certainly it wrung a kind of satiric poem out of me—Nelson Mandela as Rudolf Hess in blackface! What else can a writer do to protect his humanity against such egregious assaults! But yet again, to equate Nelson Mandela to the archcriminal Rudolf Hess is a macabre improvement on the attitude of regarding him as sub-human. It belongs on that same scale of apartheid's self-improvement as the ratio between Sharpeville and Von Brandis Square, that near-kind, near-considerate, almost benevolent dispersal of the first native-press rebellion.

That world which is so conveniently traduced by apartheid thought is of course that which I so wholeheartedly embrace—and this is my choice, among several options, of the significance of my presence here. It is a world that nourishes my being, one that is so self-sufficient, so replete in all aspects of its productivity, so confident in itself and in its destiny that it experiences no fear in reaching out to others and in responding to the reach of others. It is the hearthstone of our creative existence. It consti-tutes the prism of our world perception, and this means that our sight need not be and has never been permanently turned inward. If it were, we would not so easily understand the enemy on our doorstep or understand how to obtain the means to disarm it. When this society that is apartheid South Africa indulges from time to time in appeals to the outside world that it represents the last bastion of civilization against the hordes of barbarism from its north, we can even afford an indulgent smile. It is sufficient, imagines this state, to raise the specter of a few renegade African leaders, psychopaths and robber barons whom we ourselves are victims of, whom we denounce before the world and overthrow when we are able—this apartheid society insists to the world that its picture of the future is the reality that only its policies can erase. This is a continent that only destroys, it proclaims, a continent peopled by a race that has never contributed anything positive to the world's pool of knowledge. A vacuum that will suck into its insatiable maw the entire fruits of centuries of European civilization, then spew out the resulting mush with contempt. How strange that a society that claims to represent this endangered face of progress should itself be locked in centuries-old fantasies, should be blithely unaware of, or indifferent to, the fact that it is the last institutionally functioning product of archaic articles of faith in Euro-Judaic thought.

The God and Law, for example, especially the former. The black race has more than sufficient historic justification to be a little paranoid about the intrusion of alien deities into its destiny. For even today, apartheid's mentality of the preordained rests, according to its own unabashed claims, on what I can only describe as incidents in a testamentary Godism—I dare not call it Christianity. The sons of Ham on the one hand, the descendants of Shem on the other. The once pronounced, utterly immutable curse. As for Law, these supremacists base their refusal to concede the right of equal political participation to blacks on a claim that Africans have neither respect nor the slightest proclivity for Law—that is, for any arbitrating concept between the individual and the collective.

Even the mildest, liberal, somewhat regretful but contented apologists for apartheid, for at least some form of apartheid that is not apartheid but that ensures the status quo—even this ambivalent breed bases its case on this lack of the idea of Law in the black mind. I need only refer to a recent contribution to this literature in the form of an autobiography by a famous heart-transplant surgeon, one who in his own scientific right has probably been a candidate for a Nobel Prize in the sciences. Despite constant intellectual encounters on diverse levels, the sad phenomenon persists of Afrikaaner minds that, in the words of Eddie Roux, are products of complete acceptance of the "traditional attitudes of the time."

They have, as already acknowledged, quite "respectable" intellectual ancestors. Friedrich Wilhelm Hegel, to cite just my favorite example, found it convenient to pretend that the African had not yet developed to the level where he "attained that realization of any substantial objective existence—as for example, God or Law—in which the interest of man's volition is involved and in which he realizes his own being." He continues: "This distinction between himself as an individual and the universality of his essential being, the African in the uniform, undeveloped oneness of his existence has not yet attained: so that the knowledge of absolute Being, an Other and a Higher than his individual self, is entirely wanting." Futile to waste a moment refuting the banal untruthfulness of this claim. I content myself with extracting from it only a lesson that escapes, even today, those who insist that the pinnacle of man's intellectual thrust is the capacity to project his universality in the direction of a super-other. There is, I believe, a very healthy school of thought that not only opposes this materially but has produced effectively structured societies that operate independently of this seductive, even productively inspiring but extravagant fable.

Once we thus overcome the temptation to contest the denial of this feat of imaginative projection to the African, we find ourselves left only with the dispassionate exercise of examining in what areas we encounter differences between the histories of societies that, according to Hegel and company, never conceived of this Omnipotent Extrusion into Infinite Space, and those that did—be these differences in the areas of economic or artistic life, social relations or scientific attainment, in short, in all those activities that are empirically verifiable, quite different from the racial consequences of imprecations arising from that post-Adam-and-Eve nudist escapade in the Old Testament.

When we do this, we come upon a curious fact. The precolonial history of African societies—and I refer to both Euro-Christian and Arab-Islamic colonization—indicates very clearly that African societies never at any time in their existence went to war with another over the issue of *their* religion. That is, at no time did the black race attempt to

13

subjugate or forcibly convert others with any holier-than-thou evangelizing zeal. Economic and political motives, yes. But not religion. Perhaps this unnatural fact was responsible for the conclusions of Hegel; we do not know. Certainly the bloody histories of the world's major religions, localized skirmishes of which extend even to the present, lead to a sneaking suspicion that religion, as defined by these eminent philosophers, comes to self-knowledge only through the activity of war.

When, therefore, toward the close of the twentieth century, that is, centuries after the crusades and jihads that laid waste other and one another's civilizations, fragmented ancient cohesive social relations, and trampled upon the spirituality of entire peoples, smashing their cultures in obedience to the strictures of unseen gods—when, today, we encounter nations whose social reasoning is guided by canonical, theological claims, we believe, on our part, that the era of darkness has never truly left the world. A state whose justification for the continuing suppression of its indigenes, indigenes who constitute the majority on that land, rests on claims to divine selection is a menace to secure global relationships in a world that thrives on nationalism as common denominator. Such a society does not, in other words, belong in this modern world. We also have our myths, but we have never employed them as a base for the subjugation of others. We also inhabit a realistic world, however, and, for the recovery of the fullness of that world, the black race has no choice but to prepare itself and volunteer the supreme sacrifice.

In speaking of that world—both myth and reality—it is our duty, perhaps our very last peaceful duty to a doomed enemy, to remind it, and its supporters outside its boundaries, that the phenomenon of ambivalence induced by the African world has a very long history but that most proponents of the slanderous aspects have long ago learned to abandon the untenable. Indeed it is probably even more pertinent to remind this racist society that our African world, its cultural hoards, and its philosophical thought have had concrete impacts on the racists' own forebears, have proved seminal to a number of movements, and even created tributaries, both pure and polluted, among the white indigenes in their own homelands.

Such a variety of encounters and responses has been due, naturally, to profound searches for new directions in these people's cultural adventures, for solaces to counter the remorseless mechanization of their existence, indeed for new meanings for the mystery of life and new ways to overcome the social malaise created by the very triumphs of their own civilization. It has led to a profound respect for the African contribution to world knowledge, which did not, however, end the habitual denigration of the African world. It has created in places a near deification of the African person—that phase in which every African had to be a prince—which, yet again, was coupled with a primitive fear and loathing of the person of the African. To these paradoxical responses, the essentiality of our black being remains untouched. For the black race knows, and is content simply to know, itself. It is the European world that has sought, with the utmost zeal, to redefine itself through these encounters, even when the European has appeared to be endeavoring to grant meaning to an experience of the African world.

We can make use of the example of that period of European expressionism, a movement that saw African art, music, and dramatic rituals share the same sphere of influence as the most disparate, astonishingly incompatible collection of ideas, ideologies, and social tendencies: Freud, Marx, Bakunin, Nietzsche, cocaine, and free love. What wonder, then, that the spiritual and plastic presences of the Bakota, Nimba, the Yoruba, Dogon, Dan, and so on, should find themselves at once the inspiration and the anathematized of a delirium that was most peculiarly European, mostly Teutonic and Gallic, spanning at least four decades across the last and the present centuries. Yet the vibrant goal remained complete liberation of man, that freeing of his yet untapped potential that would carve marble blocks for the constructing of a new world, debourgeoisify existing constrictions of European thought, and light the flame to forge a new fraternity throughout this brave new world. Yes, within this single movement that covered the vast spectrum of outright fascism, anarchism, and revolutionary communism, the reality that was Africa was, as always, sniffed at, delicately tested, swallowed entire, regurgitated, appropriated, extolled, and damned in the revelatory frenzy of a continent's re-creative energies.

Oskar Kokoschka, for instance: for this dramatist and painter, African ritualism led mainly in the direction of sadism, sexual perversion, general self-gratification. It flowed naturally into a Nietzschean apocalyptic summons, full of self-induced, ecstatic rage against society, indeed, against the world. Vassily Kandinsky, on his part, responded to the principles of African art by foreseeing "a science of art erected on a broad foundation which must be international in character" and insisting that "[i]t is interesting, but certainly not sufficient, to create an exclusively European art theory." The science of art would then lead, according to him, to "a comprehensive synthesis which will extend far beyond the confines of art into the realm of the oneness of the human and the 'divine'." This same movement, whose centenary will be due for celebrations in European artistic capitals in the next decade or two, saw, among several paradoxes, the phenomenon of European artists of later acknowledged giant stature—Modigliani, Matisse, Gauguin, Picasso, Brancusi, and so on—worshiping, with varying degrees of fervor, at the shrine of African and Polynesian artistic revelations, even as Johannes Becher, in his expressionist delirium, swore to build a new world on the eradication of all plagues, including "Negro tribes, fever, tuberculosis, venereal epidemics, intellectual psychic defects—I'll fight them, vanquish them." And was it by coincidence that, contemporaneously with this stirring manifesto, yet another German enthusiast, Leo Frobenius—with no claims whatever to being part of, or indeed having the least interest in, the expressionist movement—was able to visit Ile-Ife, the heartland and cradle of the Yoruba race, and be profoundly stirred by an object of beauty, the product of the Yoruba mind and hand, a classic expression of that serene portion of the world resolution of that race. In his own words:

Before us stood a head of marvellous beauty, wonderfully cast in antique bronze, true to the life, incrusted with a patina of glorious dark green. This was, in very deed, the Olokun, Atlantic Africa's Poseidon.

Yet listen to what he had to write about the very people whose handiwork had lifted him into these realms of universal sublimity:

Profoundly stirred, I stood for many minutes before the remnant of the erstwhile Lord and Ruler of the Empire of Atlantis. My companions were no less astounded. As though we had agreed to do so, we held our peace. Then I looked around and saw—the blacks—the circle of the sons of the "venerable priest," his Holiness the Oni's friends, and his intelligent officials. I was moved to silent melancholy at the thought that this assembly of

16

degenerate and feeble-minded posterity should be the legitimate guardians of so much loveliness.

A direct invitation to a free-for-all race for dispossession, justified on the grounds of the keeper's unworthiness, it recalls other schizophrenic conditions that are mother to, for instance, the far more lethal, dark mythopoeia of Van Lvyck Louw. For though this erstwhile Nazi sympathizer would later rain maledictions on the heads of the more extreme racists of his countrymen, he said, "Lord, teach us to think what 'own' is, Lord, let us think! and then: over hate against blacks, browns, whites: over this and its cause I dare to call down judgement." Van Lvyck's powerful epic, *Raka*, was guaranteed to churn up the white cesspools of these primordial fears. A work of searing, visceral impact operating on racial memory, it would feed the Afrikaaner credo on the looming specter of a universal barbaric recession, bearing southward on the cloven hooves of the Fifth Horseman of the Apocalypse, the black.

There is a deep lesson for the world in the black races' capacity to forgive, one that, I often think, has much to do with ethical precepts that spring from their worldview and authentic religions, none of which is ever totally eradicated by the accretions of foreign faiths and implicit ethnocentrisms. For, not content with being a racial slanderer, one who did not hesitate to denigrate, in such uncompromisingly nihilistic terms, the ancestral fount of the black races—a belief that this ethnologist himself observed—Frobenius was also a notorious plunderer, one of a long line of European archaeological raiders. The museums of Europe testify to this insatiable lust of Europe; the frustrations of the ministries of culture of the Third World and of organizations like UNESCO are a continuing testimony to the tenacity, even the recidivist nature, of your routine receiver of stolen goods. Yet, is it not amazing that Frobenius is today still honored by black institutions, black leaders, and black scholars? that his anniversaries provide ready excuse for intellectual gatherings and symposia on the black continent? that his racist condescensions and assaults have not been permitted to obscure either his contribution to the knowledge of Africa or the role he has played in the understanding of the phenomenon of human culture and society, even in spite of the frequent patchiness of his scholarship?

It is the same largeness of spirit that has informed the relationship

17

today of erstwhile colonial nations, some of which have undergone the most cruel forms of settler or plantation colonialism, where a human degradation that goes with greed and exploitation attained such levels of perversion that human ears, hands, and noses served to atone for failures in production quota. Nations that underwent the agony of wars of liberation, whose earth freshly teems with the bodies of innocent victims and unsung martyrs, live side by side today with their recent enslavers, even sharing the control of their destiny with those who, barely four or five years ago, compelled them to witness the massacre of their kith and kin. Over and above Christian charity, they are content to rebuild, and share. This spirit of collaboration is easy to dismiss as the treacherous ploy of that special breed of leaders who settle for early compromises in order to safeguard, for their own use, the polished shoes of the departing oppressors. In many cases, the truth of this must be conceded. But we also have examples of regimes, allied to the aspirations of their masses on the black continent, that have adopted this same political philosophy. And, in any case, the final arbiters are the people themselves, from whose relationships any observations such as this obtain any validity. Let us simply content ourselves with remarking that it is a phenomenon worthy of note.

There are, after all, European nations today whose memory of domination by other races remains so vivid more than two centuries after liberation that a terrible vengeance culturally, socially, and politically is still exacted, even at this very moment, from the descendants of those erstwhile conquerors. I have visited such nations whose cruel histories under foreign domination are enshrined as icons to daily consciousness in monuments and parks, in museums and churches, in documentation, woodcuts, and photogravures displayed under bulletproof glass, but, most telling of all, in the reduction of the remnants of the conquering hordes to the degraded status of aliens on sufferance, with reduced civic rights, privileges, and social status, a barely tolerated marginality that expresses itself in the pathos of downcast faces, dropped shoulders, and apologetic encounters in those rare times when intercourse with the latterly assertive race is unavoidable. Yes, all this I have seen, and much of it has been written about and debated in international gatherings. And even while acknowledging the poetic justice of it in the abstract, one cannot help but wonder if a physical pound of flesh, excised at birth, is not a kinder act than a lifelong visitation of the sins of the father on the sons even to the tenth and twelfth generations.

Confronted with such traditions of attenuating the racial and cultural pride of these marginalized or minority peoples, the mind travels back to our own societies, where such causative histories are far fresher in the memory, where the ruins of formerly thriving communities still speak eloquent accusations and the fumes still rise from the scorched-earth strategies of colonial and racist myopia. Yet the streets bear the names of former oppressors, their statues and other symbols of subjugation are left to decorate their squares, the consciousness of a fully confident people having relegated them to mere decorations and roosting places for bats and pigeons. And the libraries remain unpurged, so that new generations freely browse through the works of Frobenius, of Hume, Hegel, and others, without first encountering, freshly stamped on the flyleaf: WARNING! THIS WORK IS DANGEROUS FOR YOUR RACIAL SELF-ESTEEM.

Yet these proofs of accommodation, on the grand or minuscule scale, collective, institutional, or individual, must not be taken as proof of an infinite, uncritical capacity of black patience. They constitute in their own nature a body of tests, an accumulation of debt, an implicit offer that must be matched by concrete returns. They are the blocks in a suspended bridge begun from one end of a chasm that, whether the builders will it or not, must obey the law of matter and crash down beyond a certain point, settling definitively into the widening chasm of suspicion, frustration, and redoubled hate. On that testing ground which, for us, is southern Africa, that medieval camp of biblical terrors, primitive suspicions, a choice must be made by all lovers of peace: either to bring it into the modern world, into a rational state of being within that spirit of human partnership, a capacity for which has been so amply demonstrated by every liberated black nation on our continent, or to bring it abjectly to its knees by ejecting it, in every aspect, from humane recognition, so that it caves in internally, through the strategies of its embattled majority. Whatever the choice, this inhuman affront cannot be allowed to pursue our twentieth-century conscience into the twenty-first, that symbolic coming of age which peoples of all cultures appear to celebrate with rites of passage. That calendar, we know, is not universal, but time is, and so are the imperatives of time. And of

19

those imperatives that challenge our being, our presence, and our humane definition at this time, none can be considered more pervasive than the end of racism, the eradication of human inequality and the dismantling of all its structures. The prize is the consequent enthronement of its complement: universal suffrage—and peace.

Abeokuta, Nigeria

The Phelps-Stokes Fund was founded in 1911 to administer a bequest from Caroline Phelps Stokes stipulating that the resulting income be used for the creation and improvement of housing in the City of New York for poor families, and for educational programs for Africans, Black Americans, American Indians, and needy white students. At its first official meeting, the Fund's Board of Trustees passed a resolution on "Plan and Scope" stating that the Fund would encourage publication of "investigations and reports" on matters falling within its charter and "thought to be of great significance." Ever since, publications have been central to the Fund's activities.

Among the Fund's earliest publications are pioneering surveys such as Negro Education in the United States (1912); Education in Africa (1922) and Education in East Africa (1925), the first comprehensive treatment of the subject; The Problem of Indian Administration (the "Meriam Report") (1928); The Navajo Indian Problem (1939); and Slums and Housing (1936). Other works from that period include serials such as the Phelps-Stokes Fellowship Papers published by the University of Georgia from 1913 to 1938 and by the University of Virginia from 1915 to 1936; Education, Native Welfare, and Race Relations in East and South Africa (1934); Art and the Color Line (1939); and The Atlantic Charter and Africa From an American Standpoint (1942).

In subsequent years, Fund publications include such titles as the seminal Encyclopedia of the Negro (1946), conceived and begun by Dr. W.E.B. DuBois, and the later American Negro Reference Book (1966) and The Black American Reference Book (1976); South Africa Today, by Alan Paton (1951); Housing Design: A Social Theory (1960); A History of the New York State Colonization Society (1966); United States Policy Toward Africa (1975); and more than 100 monographs, articles, and reports on educational issues and race relations in both Africa and the United States.

This volume, the third of the Occasional Papers of the Phelps-Stokes Fund, presents the text of the 1986 Nobel Literature Prize Lecture by Nigerian playwright Wole Soyinka.

Occasional Paper No. 1   The Nobel Peace Prize Lecture. Desmond M. Tutu.
Occasional Paper No. 2   Writer and Region. Athol Fugard.
Occasional Paper No. 3   This Past Must Address Its Present. Wole Soyinka.

ISBN-0-940605-03-1